Letters To The Universe

P.S. I Love You

Marie Elizabeth Manning

BookLeaf
Publishing

India | USA | UK

Made with ❤ on the BookLeaf Publishing Platform
www.bookleafpub.in
www.bookleafpub.com

Dedication

Dedicated to Glenda Sue Bixler-Harper

Thank for always seeing me and loving me

To my cousin Laura, John and Kaili

Love you

Dedication

Preface

This book is a collection of poems about my life

The experience I have gained

The challenges I have faced

The feelings I have endured

And the love I have accepted

Good or bad

This life is mine

Acknowledgements

Special Thank You

Laura Bixler

D'Shan Berry

Vladimir Anorve

Helen Walters

1. Thank you for being you

Thank you for caring
Thank you for always going the extra mile
Thank you for thinking about me with a smile
Thank you for being so self aware
And wondering if I even care
Thank you for checking in on me
Especially when sad times are surrounding
Thank you for showing up and giving things a chance
Even if you gave things a second glance
Thank you for dealing with the ups and down
And reminding me that hope can be found

To: D'Shan Berry

2. South Park

I walked around for an hour today
To put flowers on the graves of my friend's loved ones
To hear the stories they hold so dear
Celebrating laughter and shedding tears
How beautiful each life can be
All the things that make us you and me
So share those stories you hold so dear
Don't be ashamed to shed a tear
I know when I'm gone
Great stories there will be
Of how I loved hard and was a great human being

To: Grace

3. Biscuits and gravy

Aunties touch, mama bear and grandmas too
Saturday morning biscuits and gravy crew
Drop biscuits, buttery brown
Sausage gravy pepper ground
Air filled with laughter, while biscuits rise
Bellies full and satisfied
How I miss those morning memories
Of family time so gleefully
We share the recipes and say amen
To biscuits, gravy and our kin

To: The Bixlers

4. Red Beans, Rice and Sausage

Well slap your mama if it tastes too good
My taste buds dance, just like they should
Cooking up supper and don't think twice
Add the bay leaf and a dash of spice
Louisiana style
Green chili corn bread with cheese
Just like Auntie made on a Sunday please
Nothing like the smell of home in just one dish
Oh my, a second helping is all I wish

To: Aunt Glenda

5. Fanny May

I am my mother's daughter
Strong, wise, witty and free
Everything I am, she created so carefully
She looked into the stars
And made a special wish
That I would be her baby
She sealed it with a kiss
Every single tear
Every single loss
Prepared her life for me
My siblings that wait in heaven
I just can't wait to meet
Thank you mom for life
And all the endless love
From your beautiful daughters
We are everything you dreamed of

To: My Mama

6. Candy Land

Why are you so tasty and sweet
Good enough to rot my teeth
Caramel, nugget and peanut butter
Too many sweets will cause you trouble
Bunch Oh Crunch
100 Grand
Almond Joys
Share with a friend
Pink cotton candy
When I was young
Would leave me happy, with a red tongue

To: My Sweet Tooth

7. Nashville

Nashville Hot Chicken
Ole Smoky Moonshine shots
Walking down Broadway feeling all the country and
rock
Ryman auditorium tours
Sing-along to songs at Tootsies bar
Wandering museums
Hoping to see a star
Stumble upon a tiki lounge
And music fills the air
Some dreams do come true
In Tennessee, I do declare

To: Shelby

8. The Fosters

Aunt Beth and Uncle Rick
The parents I never had
The place that always felt like home
Keebler elf cookies
Pool side coconut oil tans
Remembering the good times
And remembering the sad
Battle scars that linger
The people who understand
Celebrating the good times
Processing the bad
Memaws pickle recipe
Chocolate Fudge pie for holidays
Mr.Magoo's potatoes
And love that never fades

To: Beth & Rick

9. The Hurricane

You irritate me

You are a dream crusher

You are a menace to society

The love I feel for the people you have taken is all

consuming

Every year I walk for hope

I jump for joy

I remember what a blessing they all were

You are just a lonely demon that doesn't deserve an once

of my energy

I just want you to know I will always fight

Always lift up

Always remember

You can keep going through lives like a hurricane

But I stand strong

I cry hard

And never waiver from telling you how much you suck

To: To Every Cancer Warrior

10. Miguelito

Flaming Hot Cheetos
Ramen noodle cups
Little Caesars pizza
Watching you grow up
Little baby brother
Growing into a man
No one can prepare you
For how life can take a bend
Tragic loss with sorrow
Thinking of you with love
Little baby brother
With our Lord above
Never once are you forgotten
In our hearts you will remain
Celebrating each memory
So they will never fade

To: Letty

11. Friends Forever

Unconditional
Cries and lies
Stick with me, your alibi
All I want is a friend
One that doesn't love to pretend
Always here
Always waiting
Throw a bone
A lifeline taken
Olive branches
Compromise
Lonely girl until I die

To: My Inner child

12. All Alone

In my head is where I live
It's not always safe, something's got to give
Overthink and overwhelmed
Sometimes I live in a fiery hell
Broken, lost and all alone
The darkness covers me head to toe
Engulfed in flames
I burn alive
A sweet life never satisfied
The burden that lives inside of me
Imprinted in the family tree

To: Breaking the cycle

13. The Game

Do you want to hold my hand
Or am I just the lust you love
Would you tell people I'm your girl
Or am I just a secret place holder
Do you really think of me
Or am I just good in bed
Does the thought of me make you smile
Or am I just too available
Would you marry me
Would you stand by my side
Or do you just like the way I taste
Would you build a life with me
Be mine, my love, my king
Or do we just keep playing this game

To: The temptation

14. The Two Way Street

Why do I insist
On being so considerate
Why do I love chasing after you
Maybe I need a friend
Or maybe just trying to feel un-blue
I want you to feel
As loved as you can be
When you feel uneasy
I can feel it inside of me
The more and more I try
Everyone fades away
No calls
No texts
No birthday cards
To keep that blues away

To: My consideration

15. Dancing Light

Spirit names
Sweat lodges with pine
Vision quests under full moons
The beat of the drums
Footprints in time
Peace connecting everything
Love intertwined
Send well wishes to Mother Earth
Praise Grandfather Sky
Grandmother Moon watches over our dreams
Sister Sunrise brings a new day
Wizard Wells
Sacred ground
Connected to my ancestors
And knowing who I am

To: Wizard Wells Texas

16. Heaven

I wonder what heaven is like
If I die tomorrow
Do you think I'll arrive
Have I been good
Have I been nice
Let go of resentments
And just live my life
The love of God and Jesus
Runs through my veins
But demons infect the thoughts inside my brain
Peace ever lasting
Washes away all that is bad
Let him into my heart
Know he's there when I'm sad
I wonder if it feels like a mother's love
To make it to heaven
In the clouds up above

To: My Faith

17. Lover Girl

To be loved is to feel seen
To remember what you like
Just to set the scene
Making you feel wanted
Nothing left to lose
Letting go enough
To be with the one who loves you
Never fight the fall
Just to be unseen
Love creates wonders
The peace inside of me
Waiting, wanting
Forever more
Love comes knocking at my door

To: The One

18. The Path

This road I take
Is dark and cold
Finding myself
Learning to grow
Friends fading fast
Alone on my path
Glorious horizon
Lonely road
Everlast
Building a future
That touches the sky
Sacrifice Serenade
While gathering my pride

To: My Career

19. Glory to God

Protect and Praise
Glory to God
Filled with grace
Endless mercy surrounding me
Inside my heart
His love always lives
For all my blessings
He gives and gives
With peace like light calming me
I walk hand in hand
So blessed to be
Above all else
You are father God
Above the stars to see it all

To: Father God

20. Movie Madness

Movies are so comforting
Comedies, adventures and documentaries
Escape from life
A good plot twist
Animations from childhood
That taught me humble things
Rudolph the Red Nose Reindeer specials
On a snowy Christmas Eve
Horror movies that make me scream
Popcorn buttery and warm
Chocolate covered almonds
Dollar movies
Couldn't ask for more

To: Allen Theaters

21. It's My Party

I can cry
I can pout
I can blow my candles out
I can make a wish come true
Eat some cake and pizza too
Laughter in the corners of my brain
Friends and family celebrate
How good it feels to be me
To be born
So blessed be
My life hand picked from God
One day to reflect it all
Celebrate who you are or even cry
Another year
Life passing by

To: November

www.ingramcontent.com/pod-product-compliance
Lightning Source LLC
Chambersburg PA
CBHW051002030426
42339CB00007B/452